SETH

A
Multidimensional
Autobiography

Seth Returns Publishing
Lake County California

Published by Seth Returns Publishing
Lake County California

Editorial: Mark Allen Frost
Cover Art, Design, Typography & Layout: Mark Frost

Library of Congress Control Number: 2011902589

ISBN: 978-0-9826946-3-3

This book is dedicated to all of Seth's readers,

past, present, and future. Special thanks to Carol Joy

for assistance with editing and Richard Strauss for

technical help in the production of this book.

CONTENTS

PREFACE

Hello everyone. Welcome to our new project. A moment... As an educator to humankind for many years, I have had the opportunity to notice when and by what means my Teachings to those of you in the Third Dimension are actually understood and utilized. Much of this material I present to you does indeed go "over your head." By this I mean, that, I perhaps use descriptive phrases that are not necessarily relevant to the average reader. I have learned my Lesson, however, and I promise to you in this current manuscript that I shall attempt to keep the discourse on an elementary to intermediate level. We shall save the "expert testimony," a humorous phrase I believe, for the audience that LOVES the intellectual hair-splitting aspect of my works.

These are simply some of the countless lives of the Seth Entity, chosen for their inherent qualities of illustrating the strengths, deficits, and typical Lessons of lives. All of the Soul Family members will not be identified in all cases, for reasons of privacy. In one case, however, we have allowed you a peek at the specifics regarding Soul

Family incarnations in time. This would be the Indian Existence.

So I ask you to enjoy this little project of ours for what it is: an entertainment, primarily. But also we would hope that you will attempt YOUR OWN survey of some of your own lives. It may be enlightening.

Overview

Your culture is interested in personality,
first and foremost...

Body of Work

Mark: Seth - A Multidimensional Autobiography. Is there anything you would like to add to this, Seth?

Seth: Yes, just to confirm that it was I, Seth, who "inspired" you to come up with the idea of an autobiography... the work will pull together our other volumes into one coherent "body" of work; *(humorously)* a survey if you wish. And you are quite correct in your feelings, I believe, that your culture is interested in personality, first and foremost. I am hoping with this personality piece to help the world community on the journey inward, toward the Soul Self of the individual.

This can be a tricky endeavor, Mark. You have already noticed in our work together that I use this technique of distracting the reader with interesting bits of ephemera while I deliver Soul-based material to the unconscious. This shall continue in the biography in a format suited for the masses, again, as we presented in the 9/11 book. I will ask you to keep your intellect out of the mix here. In matters of catalyzing the human spirit to look within and simply BEGIN the spiritual journey, we must keep it very, very elementary.

We are appealing to the subconscious, here, as you well know. This aspect of consciousness is much concerned with symbols and basic concepts of manifestation. The emotional expression on this level is also quite basic. Of course, the ego/intellect is nowhere to be found. Communications with All That Is stream into the portal between the eyes on a moment-to-moment basis. The human is informed by the Divine always. We will be attempting to assist the reader in discovering this in our book.

As I discuss my perspective and my existences it will be as a way, Mark, for our interested, INVOLVED readers – note my emphasis – to continue on the journey of Soul Evolution and self-exploration. It has appeal on many levels. A curiosity piece, if you will. But again, I will be teaching the Lessons on the subtle levels while entertaining the reader on the physical. Now, let us have some dictation…

OVERVIEW

Multidimensional Experiencing

My beginnings are yours, Dear Reader. I was born from consciousness, the Loving consciousness of All That Is. I have lived many lives upon the Earth, upon other planetary bodies within your Universe, and within other systems of reality.

You are in a similar position as I, however, in that YOU TOO are living and have lived countless lives within these identical environments that I have just listed. The difference here between us, is that I Seth am now inhabiting an etheric body - a Light Body - having reached the end, you might say, of my journey into physical reality.

My perspective is one of multidimensional experiencing of ALL of my past, present, and future existences, in your terms. I am not bound by the linear time constraints of your camouflage reality, you see, and so I may freely explore, from within the full moment of my awareness, the minutiae, if you will, of any particular existence.

These lives of mine include fully-embodied lives in which, for instance, I lived as a seagoing human, a man with lusty appetites and a predilection for strong drink, as well as a life within the French Colonial period as a female of high estate.

I have lived lives of great wealth and great poverty also. I have been of the benevolent persuasion as well as the opposite of this perspective. Throughout my tenure as a human being, the Seth Entity has created many interesting lifetimes of learning.

Your Very Human Tendency

Now… though I am, at this stage of my development, quite adverse to airing my "dirty laundry," as you put it, I also realize that it is often the sensationalist bits of gossip that serve to fuel much of your popular media. I am not necessarily referring to the Negative Media with this, I am merely commenting upon your very human tendency to dig up the dirt on your fellows, your fellow humans, you see. I shall indulge your tastes in this matter, therefore.

I must agree that it is indeed quite a bit more entertaining to hear of the adventurous, though perhaps tawdry exploits, of the vivacious liver of life, than to suffer through the mono-tonal narrative describing the life barely lived.

Individual Human Input

Now Mark, let us create some outlined lives here. We shall have several chapters dealing with different lives. What I hope to accomplish is to demonstrate how each of these lives are quite part-and-parcel to the times in which they were lived. I will certainly attempt to explain for the reader how they too are part-and-parcel of their timeframe of existence. Each of you, you see, is a very necessary part of the Consensus Reality in which you live. Your world on all of its many levels WOULD NOT EXIST without your individual human input into the creation of your Personal Reality Field.

Linear Time

It seems as though we are back in the book. Let us use these asides as a part of this book, Mark. I do like the immediacy generated with this technique.

Mark: OK Seth. I like it too.

Seth: Yes Mark, now in answer to your telepathic inquiry, I do not believe we shall cover lives already described in the old material. Those lives are already on the record and I do not wish to duplicate material here. I would like to include the lives we discussed recently in which all of us: Jane, Rob, you Mark as well as Cas, experienced our Indian existences. So we shall have the ancient Indian existence of Seth, perhaps to open up the section of the book on the lives lived, in sequence now. Not necessarily in linear time sequence, if you get my meaning.

Mark: I don't really.

Seth: Mark we will attempt to demonstrate the non-linear nature of existence by describing lives that were lived at different points in your history, within your present timeframe i.e., one of your Simultaneous Lives that you are living currently, as well as FUTURE lives. This will stimulate the reader to explore their own multidimensional existence. At least, that is the goal here. Do you follow me?

Mark: Yes Seth. We are going to make it interesting and inspiring.

Seth: That is nicely put, Mark. Now… The ancient Far East Indian existence will be followed by a future existence, one that is now, at this time, *(humorously)* occurring in probability, a probable existence. This female IS living within an advanced society that reaches its zenith around 4018 AD. Many new developments in all of the domains of existence are being experienced by this human, and we will pull the reader in with this material.

Fragments of Consciousness

I believe we should, for your education as well as the reader's, cover your personality fragment existence that I have recently revealed to you, Mark, in which you placed a part of your Soul Self within the consciousness of a female living within your New Orleans. If you remember, this action on the part of your higher self set the stage for future meetings with the progeny of this female, by you Mark, in your current existence. We will demonstrate the flexibility of consciousness with this life.

Following up on my statement of long ago that I at one time projected a fragment of my consciousness into an animal upon your Earth to experience life from that vantage point, we shall briefly describe that process. I believe we might connect this discussion to tribal magic, the transmigration of Souls, that sort of thing.

Mark, it seems we may have a bit more than several descriptions of lives for this volume. I am picking up on your ideas in this matter and I do agree that we would do well to round out the selection with a few more short examples.

Other Systems

I use the phrase "in other systems" quite often in the new messages. I think it would be appropriate, therefore, to relate to the reader some of my experiences in systems of reality that are quite foreign to the average human. These systems exist in other dimensions, including the Fourth and Fifth Dimensions, in an entirely novel context. The Home Dimension and the various intermediary dimensions are included here. We should briefly touch on these lives, though perhaps we should refer to them as Post Transition lives, or some such description.

Beyond these afterdeath realities exist environments that the Soul visits for learning purposes. I have told you recently of the dimension where Love is experienced as the primary emotional state. There is no negativity here. It is not allowed. There is a dimension of experience, also, in which perfection, as you understand it, is experienced.

As you know, the Soul sends parts of itself into multiple environments of experiencing to receive the breadth of Value Fulfillment it requires to evolve, or perhaps expand would be a more appropriate term, though I do not wish to spark the discussion of expanding or contracting universes here. Perhaps we should stick with our term of evolution, Soul Evolution.

Seth: Would you please assemble an outline from these notes, with my assistance of course?

Mark: Sure. Will you follow the format of opening with Introductions, a section on the basic concept of the work and a Preface?

Seth: No, I believe we can trim these components from this volume. We are creating a slim volume here. I believe we can safely dispense with the Introductions and the Concept Page. Perhaps a brief Preface, one page will do. If we do indeed decide to include the asides and our conversations in this manuscript, the Introductions and other pieces we used in our past books would appear superfluous. Please find a better term here Mark.

Mark: Unnecessary?

OVERVIEW

Seth: Excellent! We are streamlining our presentation here, Mark, to appeal to the tastes of the average human "on the go." The Fourth-Dimensional Shift is well underway for all of you. Time is speeding up. You do not have the patience, I am guessing, for trudging through extraneous narratives. You may also find another word for extraneous, if you wish.

Mark: Unnecessary?

Seth: Very amusing, Mark. Now the outline? Let us have several more chapters, opening with the Preface of course. The chapters will be followed by an Epilogue of one page. I do feel that in these short volumes of ours, The Trilogy, the Death Book, and others, that we should have a rather extensive Glossary. Now Mark, we will not have an index, as you know, I find these additions to be unnecessary *(humorously)* in my new works. The books will be no more than 100 to 150 pages each. An index will not be necessary. Now though it was a good idea to use the large type for our books on the awakening, I believe we may now use the common size, the smaller size for the remaining works. This is one way to mark the departure from the first three books. We will be moving on, in a sense, as humanity moves forward in its evolution. We are simply documenting the progression of Evolutionary Consciousness, as I have told you before.

This consciousness is quite fluid as it creates the personality of the human being. For this reason, any discussion of my lives must include descriptions of members of the Seth Entity who exist with me as members of the Soul Family group, as we are calling it. Mark, Cas, and Jane Roberts are members of this group as are Robert Butts - the scribe of the old Seth material - and a quite varied assortment of people throughout the ages, past, present, and future.

No Boundaries

The personality has no real boundaries. Though you may feel as though you are contained within your own conscious, thinking mind, and within your skin and bones, you are, in truth, without boundaries of any kind. You are composed of the same material as the window, the door, the air before your eyes. The Consciousness Units (CU's) that compose all of your reality are each connected one to another. The personality of the reader is conjoined with the personality of the family pet, of the sofa in the living room, of all material and non-material substance within the personal reality.

Mystery Civilizations

Naturally we will include the Atlantean existence that many of us in our current Soul Family participated in, for I understand how you yearn for information from that life. I believe we shall expand on all of the material in the book, in an attempt to be comprehensive.

In an attempt to illustrate the pervasiveness of the human consciousness within physical reality, we will describe the process of projections of consciousness. Many of you, when you are in nature, for example, quite literally embody the elemental consciousness of the tree, the flower, the stone. You are not "taking over" the elemental entities here. You are lending your support spontaneously to the manifestation of these entities.

Becoming the Earth

Additionally, as we have hinted at the consensus manifestation of world realities in the Third Book, we will describe the process of the human quite literally, again, becoming the Earth herself – your Mother Earth. This is an example of how consciousness expands, evolves you see. Many of you do this quite often throughout your day, without truly realizing the remarkable perspective you are embodying when you do so. Typically, you think of yourself as merely quite "grounded" for that moment in time. Indeed, you are literally the ground on which you stand as well as all of the other elements that lend support to the creation of your system.

Mark: Seth, are you reconsidering the size of the book? If you wish to include a Mystery Civilization existence in the book, that would add to its length.

Seth: Mark, you are quite right here. Though I believe that we should still keep to our 100 to 150 page limit. I envision these smaller volumes as "pocketbooks" that the reader may keep on their person as they go about their day. These will be handy reference works, in other words. Certainly not weighty tomes of encyclopedic breadth: merely summaries of my key concepts.

The Indian Existence

*The loving bonds were very strong,
and we nurtured one another...*

Soul Family Life

Now... in the Far East Indian Existence, as I told you in a personal session, you and I as well as Cas, Butts and others in our collective Soul Family, lived our lives within a poor family. I was the mother here. You were a male, a sibling of Butts who was also a male. Cas was your sister in this ancient existence. As it is with all manifestations of Soul Family collectives over time, others lived their lives as part of our extended family - local merchants, aunts, uncles, nieces - who are, of course, now in your CURRENT existence, living their lives as part of your extended family, your Soul Family. Your current mate Carol, was my husband here in this Indian life.

A Jungle Existence

We were quite poor in this family. However, the loving bonds were very strong, and we nurtured one another, as loving families do. This was a jungle existence for us. Primarily, our wealth, what there was of it, came from raising goats. Our problem was an ongoing one of protecting our animals from poachers and from jungle animals. We lived in a small village of less than one hundred people. There was a river that served as our transportation network to neighboring villages several miles downstream.

The rainy season was the most difficult time for us, as the relentless downpours would inevitably break the weak points in the thatched roof of our small house. The warm weather months were spent gathering fruits and root vegetables in the surrounding jungle.

Each of us in the family had our job to do, in so far as finding and preparing foods. We also felt obliged to provide one of our goats for the village religious celebrations. As I said, this was a simple loving existence we enjoyed. Family conflicts were kept to a minimum. It was thought to be an affront to the gods to argue amongst family members. This was also how we kept the children disciplined, by reminding them of their obligation to obey the holy scriptures.

Deadly Fever

This life occurred in the 900's AD. At that time, I lived a very short life as the mother, dying in my 30's of complications from childbirth. The child was also lost. Now my husband immediately took on another mate to help support the family. The period for grieving was short, therefore, as the rainy season was beginning.

My husband, the reincarnation of your wife Carol, Mark, died at 42 of an infection he received from insect bites. It was a slow and painful death for him. He was comforted by his new wife and she would take on a new husband almost immediately on the death of the old one. The sons were to grow into healthy adults who married young and raised families of their own. The raising of goats was our practice and so the sons carried on that business and did quite well. The sons, including you, died in their 40's just as their father did. They contracted a deadly fever from insect bites and quickly succumbed in the same year.

Analysis:

What was learned here, for the individuals and for the Entity? Specifically, for the individuals involved, an appreciation for the basic loving family unit was learned and honored during this existence. There were also Lessons of subsistence, Lack, making do with what one has, and so on. This tendency to settle for what is, rather than strive for what may be, makes itself known over the generations into the present manifestation of humans in your modern world. Mark, for example, if I may so bold, *(humorously)* has a notable characteristic of personality that he exhibits, in which he limits himself, thinking he does not deserve great abundance. He is often at these times experiencing bleedthroughs to this other existence in which he and his family merely subsisted on the Earth. The experiences of this poor family act to present to Mark and other members of his Soul Family, ways of behaving, thinking, and imagining, that limit the perception of abundance, you see, what we refer to as the Abundant Universe in the books.

Part of Awakening

Mark knows what I am speaking of here. We are certainly not discounting the valuable Lessons learned in this past existence concerning love of family and dedication to the family unit. However, I have suggested to him that it is part of his awakening in this current lifetime to create prosperity for himself and his family. Now, as we describe these other lives in the ensuing chapters, I will explain to which lives he might turn for messages of abundance and prosperity.

Dear Reader, you also have these lives within your consciousness that "help" to limit you and your expression. All of you have lived lives of great poverty as well as great wealth. Your subconscious focus on the chosen lives from your perceived past determines the general outcome of your life in your current expression.

When I suggest, for example, that the student senses a particular Feeling-Tone that they associate with a beneficial state of consciousness, this is what I mean, this is where it comes from. To be sure, on the surface, a feeling of impending good luck, or wealth does seem to come "from nowhere," as they say. Yet my suggestion to you, is that these Feeling-Tones representing positive states of consciousness can be sought after in your meditations when you intentionally visit these other lives of yours. If you have read my new books, you have received precise instructions on how to do this in a Loving and intentional way. In a sense, you are "harvesting" these positive and productive states of consciousness from these other lives so that you may make use of them in your current existence.

Cut and Paste

Another metaphor that we enjoy is "cut and paste." By journeying to your other lives and bringing back with you these positive states of consciousness, you are effectively cutting or perhaps copying the positive healing states and pasting them into your current existence. You are reformatting your current life on a "higher" level, if you will, on a level of improved Reality Creation. That is my soapbox moment for this chapter. Thank you for bearing with me.

DonRa - 4018 AD

She is anticipating a pregnancy
in her immediate future...

Fourth-Dimensional Awareness

Seth: If you would, please read to me the section that you wish to work on this morning and I will begin the transmission of the material. Is this an appropriate method?

Mark: I did sense that you were thinking of adding to the probable future existence of the female living in 4018? Would that be OK?

Seth: Mark, please notice how I am bringing you deeper for this transmission. I would like to invite you to embody this future existence of ours somewhat, so that you may more fully comprehend these Simultaneous Lives. You are deepening now. (pause)

Fourth-Dimensional awareness is your ongoing perspective in this life we are living. Additionally, we are quite able to go within, to the non-physical world, and through meditation and other technologies, access any of our lives that we wish, for study and research and for entertainment. Fourth-Dimensional awareness entails the moment-to-moment perception of the creation of realities from ideas, images, and emotions. The beliefs, your beliefs, Mark, my beliefs as your counterpart in The Entity, are clearly recognized as the broad plans for which the creation of all Reality Constructs are used by consciousness. Beliefs of all kinds, including the core beliefs that support the maintenance of your camouflage reality, are easily changed to facilitate the attainment of specific Reality Creation goals.

To Produce Offspring

Now: a moment… DonRa is the chosen name for this human, a female, as I said, of 46 years on Earth. She is anticipating a pregnancy in her immediate future. She is planning the details of this venture as to personality characteristics, temperament, and so on, that she wishes her forthcoming child to exhibit.

This is a pleasant exercise for our relative, Mark. Though the romantic love rituals of courtship that occupy you in modern times have been abandoned, for the most part, the desire to create a union with another human being to produce offspring, still holds the traditional joys and anticipations with which your species is famil-iar. This human is deciding on the appropriate character-istics for the forthcoming child that will allow them to successfully experience the life they are to live.

Our subject DonRa has "foresight," here, with re-gards to the broad agenda of experiencing for her child. She is witnessing the day-to-day experiences of her cur-rent existence, remember, as she is also experiencing the specifics of any one or all of her ongoing Reincarnational Existences. She is well aware, therefore, of her child's probable futures, as well as her own.

Mother's Love

Now this is quite so on all levels, if I may add to this description. Remember that Soul Family members incarnate in different bodies, of different sexes, personalities, and so on, lifetime after lifetime. Can you see, then, how it would be advantageous for this woman to receive information from a future Reincarnational Existence or probable existence of the child, the as yet unborn child's other lives, in other words? The mother's love is just as intense and pervading the psyche of this probable counterpart of ours, as it is within the consciousness of any mother throughout history. The mother wants the best for the child. Period. In this future existence, it is possible for the mother to put together a "birth package," so to speak, that will feed the various desired attributes into the egg and sperm and the developing fetus, to produce the desired results: in this case, a human that will most easily achieve a successful life experience on Earth.

Dreaming the Child

You might say that DonRa is "dreaming the child into being." On the etheric levels, in the dreamstate, during Astral Travels to other dimensions while in the waking state, she is consciously seeing to the manifestation of her child, first within the pre-manifestation domains in the form of a Gestalt of Consciousness having the desired characteristics, and then "later," in the manifestation into physical reality on the Earth plane. You may think of these endeavors as sacred visualizations and rituals, keyed to the specifics, as I said, of the anticipated birth and existence of the human.

This dreaming of the child into existence has a long history within your race. Many of our readers who are mothers may now be experiencing a touch of deja vu as I describe these activities of DonRa. This is the way it works for you, you see. This is the natural way. Unfortunately, you are encouraged to forget the old ways and instead, adopt the medical model as the normal method. The metaphysical aspects of pregnancy and birth have given way to science. It is all biological and surgically clean for you now.

Soul Family Negotiation

What is occurring here is this: the negotiation process begins among Soul Family members the instant that a Soul decides on the next existence. The Soul Self perceives from its vantage point in the Home Dimension, then, the potential existence before it. This would be the future existence of the baby of our DonRa. Our Soul Self, Mark, observes through holographic scenarios the basics of this life - from babyhood through adulthood and even into old age and the Transition - to get a sense of the Lessons to be covered in that lifetime. This is the main concern for Souls, as you know: the journey into the physical body is primarily for the experiencing of the Lessons of consciousness in human form.

And so these two Soul Family members - the dreaming mother and the Home Dimension aspect of the future potential baby - are communicating on the subtle levels about whether to commit themselves to the relationship, the general trajectory of development of both parties in the future, that type of thing.

An agreement is made to explore these relationships together. Our counterpart in the future is consciously participating in this negotiation. She has developed precise criteria for the manifestation of the child into physical reality, and is, in a sense, negotiating with herself – with her higher self, if you will – as to these specific ground rules for development.

Atlantis Connection

Before we move forward to comment on the birth and development of the child, let me briefly discuss the similarities that exist between this future civilization which DonRa inhabits, and the civilization from your perceived past that you refer to as Atlantis. The two collective manifestations are quite similar, for they are each founded on one another through bleedthroughs. As your best-case-scenario manifestation that you call the New World is a bleedthrough phenomenon to the ancient matriarchy GA, this progressed civilization is a bleedthrough to your Atlantean civilization. This telepathic assimilation of thought, image, and emotion between collectives is a two-way street. It works out of time within the spacious moment. *(See diagram page 150 in 911 book. mf)*

This is why I have often stated that the collective you know as Atlantis is based on reincarnational memories from your past AND from your future: memories from your future, if you may grasp that conundrum.

Multidimensional Existence

Now, regarding the birth and development of this child. A moment... As an astute reader of my new material *(humorously)* you are, no doubt, aware of my new updating of the families of consciousness material. We now describe a Soul Family collective as your vehicle, in a sense, that you use to work out your Issues and learn your Lessons in ALL of your Simultaneous Lives. We have said that for the average Soul Family member, this process is largely unconscious. The amnesia of the ego/ intellect prevents you, for the most part, from discerning the processes involved in this learning of Lessons. Here, however, thousands of years in your perceived future, DonRa, our example, is well aware of the myriad of mental and spiritual processes that occur for her as she experiences her life of Lessons. The Unity of Consciousness dimension has been revealed to humanity at this future date and everyone everywhere is now comfortable with multidimensional existence.

For example: our subject is quite able to observe before her, the very thoughts, images, and emotions that she uses to create realities. She is able to slow down her manifestation process to witness the creation of realities in her current moment. This woman is not blown away, as you say, by the intensity of imagery and emotion she experiences in the creative moment. She can handle it, she can direct it, she can easily participate in the conscious co-creation of her physical world, including, remember, every atom that composes every reality construct within her Personal Reality Field. Having been initiated, in a sense, into this elevated perceptual reality of the Fourth Dimension, this woman also can conceive before her, as though projected onto a massive screen, you see, the probable birth and ongoing life of her baby-to-be.

You might call this exercise a visualization, yet it is no ordinary visualization. She is creating not a virtual reality, here, but a literal reality. Her vision has the full features of Reality Constructs in the Third Dimension. She is creating this holographic entity as a way to get information on what she may expect if she were to go forward with dreaming the child into being. This human wishes for the child a happy, healthy, spiritually-informed existence. And so she, in a sense, enters this data into the divine program, and it is instantaneously projected into her Personal Reality for viewing and editing.

Instant Manifestation

This capacity for instant manifestation that awaits you in your future, can be compared to the creative pursuits of your artists. Of course you are all artists of 3D Reality, in that you create your realities out of the stuff of

Consciousness Units. In the Fourth Dimension, however, you will not experience the lag-time between thought and manifestation that you currently observe. As Reality Creators in the Fourth Dimension, you will witness your mental environments projected instantly onto the screen of your perceived reality, your Personal Reality Field. If you have a predominance of hateful thoughts within your consciousness, you will instantly perceive the products of those thoughts within your world. If you have a predominance of Love and compassion within your consciousness, you will observe the instantaneous manifestation ensue of these positive states of consciousness.

Now when I say that our subject DonRa presents her proposed reality before her for possible editing, I am describing a different type of perspective for you-the-reader. For example: currently, if you make a mistake in your conversation with a friend, and insult them or anger them in some way, it happens immediately. There is no going back after the careless comment, let us say. You may apologize, possibly, or in other ways attempt to smooth over the hurt feelings. You are editing your creation when you do this. You are perfecting it, making it better, you see.

Consider now the same occurrence in this future existence I am describing. You let slip a thoughtless comment, your friend is angered, you apologize as you did in the earlier example, but here there is a difference. Whereas before, in your 3rd-Dimensional experiencing, your friend might not accept your apology but pretend to do so, in effect, creating a resentment to mull over in the future, in the instant manifestation of the 4th Dimension, your apology will carry the full weight of your mani- festation powers. Your friend will be able to perceive your ultimate honesty in the apology. There will be no doubt. There will be no resentment, for your friend will see the instant manifestation of their thoughts, images, and emotions with regards to their part in the interac- tions: forgiveness, let us say. Because negative thoughts have negative consequences, in the Fourth-Dimensional awareness humans will be very careful to correct any negative manifestations as they occur. This you may a call a sense of correcting or editing "in process," while the creation is unfolding.

Analysis:

This probable future existence of the Seth Entity demonstrates for the reader, the way in which the human on Earth creates the Personal Reality. Your current momentary existence BRIDGES the past TO the future. You create your life by choosing from unlimited probabilities, those you wish to manifest in the current moment.

Now admittedly, it is a stretch of the imagination to consider the specifics of what is being created by DonRa two millennia in your perceived future. In order to grasp this, you would have to truly understand the meaning of time in your system. As I have told Mark on several occasions, ultimately, "There is no time." It is a convenience for you, as a Soul in a physical body. To sense the truth of my statement, you would need to imagine yourself OUTSIDE of time. This is my perspective. This is how I can relate to you the specifics of DonRa's life.

Additionally, please remember that all probabilities are explored by consciousness in all instances. This is true, such that, for example, your decision to read this section of our little book, represents a chosen probable path for you-the-reader, that continues on its own distinct path of development. However, had you instead decided NOT to read this section, and watched television instead, this un-chosen probable behavior of reading this section would still set into motion the un-folding of the future reality, and all that it entails. Both probable trajectories of development would continue to evolve in their own idiosyncratic ways, infinitely, up to the year 4018 and beyond, you see. All probabilities are explored,

Dear Reader. If you get anything from this example of Seth lives, please comprehend this fact of your creaturehood.

Tibetan Scribe

He approached his life as a sacred journey...

The Perennial Philosophy

The afterdeath journey of the Soul is quite well demonstrated in the rituals and observances of the Tibetan Buddhist Tradition. Our life we have lived as a young priest/student named Thingpa, reminded us, Mark, that the Soul lives on after the death of the physical body. The various stages of enlightenment that one experiences on the Transition from the physical to the etheric are noted in Tibetan Buddhism and roughly parallel the material I have given to you Mark, to Cas, and to Rob and Jane.

Do you see how this Tibetan life exists as an example of a Seth Entity Human Counterpart engaged in the translation of divine information into written texts? The Seth Teaching, the Teachings of the Buddha and other spiritual masters, have similarities, for we are all talking about the same thing. The perennial philosophy is literally true, you see. And so, in the same way that Mr. Huxley - a member of our extended family, remember - noted how the elements of this philosophy inspired him, as well as his communications with his Energy Personality and with myself, this young priest eagerly wrote down the dictation from his Guides with just as much conviction and urgency.

It was around 400 AD that this fellow created his brief, intense life of learning and study. He took vows of celibacy on entering his course of study. Previously, however, as a young man, an attractive youth in his village, he did experience what you might call the physical delights of the flesh, and so did not feel as though he was giving up much of anything.

He felt himself "destined" to act as scribe, student, priest from a very early age and when he "sowed his oats" he did so with a feeling of duty to the cause in which he was about to engage.

Remembering

Within his collective he was in deep connection to Soul. After his physical birth, for example, he retained many memories of previous lives and remembered also the contracts with All That Is that he negotiated in his Home Dimension. This fellow knew what he had to do and he approached his life as a sacred journey. He was, he felt, to assist his collective in remembering and honoring the spiritual practices of his ancestors. This was the highest calling to which he could aspire.

As I said, this fellow was connected to his past lives. He was what we have called in our manuscripts the "magical child," in that he also had prophetic powers. He knew, for example, what would occur in the future of his group. This is good information for leaders to have, I'm sure you would agree. And so our family member, this young man, served as the visionary and the scribe for his collective.

He greatly enjoyed hiking in the mountains surrounding the monastery. Oftentimes he would take provisions with him and camp out on a precipice overlooking the valley below. During these ritual journeys, he communicated with his ancestors and Guides and received inspiration for the work he was doing at the time. On return to the monastery from his ritual quests, our friend would be highly-energized and in great spirits, ready to continue with his activities.

Now the Seth Entity lives generally hold to these principles. They are generally well aware of their mission in the existence. Though that is not to say that some do not resist the calling. Some indeed do resist and I shall remark on this phenomenon when I describe the growth of Mark into the scribe for the Seth Entity.

Analysis:

Mark: Seth, could you speak about the differences, if any, between your incarnations and mine.

Seth: Now this is a very valid question. We do not wish to confuse the reader. Let us therefore establish just what we mean when we say incarnation, Simultaneous Existence, and so on.

To begin, each of you represents a spark of All That Is - the cosmologically vast creative source that gives birth to all realities. This All That Is represents the sum of Consciousness Units within the Universes. Now over time, through the millennia, you see, humans come into physical form and create lives for themselves. Each thought, behavior, image, emotion considered by each human seeks out manifestation of itself in the 3rd Dimension or others. As they do, they, in a sense, "find" one another, and assemble into electromagnetic propensities, representing potential action, behavior, image, emotion within consciousness. These Gestalts of Consciousness underlie not only your own developing existence, but also the enduring existence of everything: of rocks, of air, and so on. Everything has life, consciousness.

Because each human develops in a singular way, entertaining singular thoughts, images, and emotions, they individually feed these GOCs with their "personal material," you might say. Now there are similarities in thought and behavior that have developed as consciousness differentiates itself in the physical dimension. These differences fuel different GOCs, so that, the entirety of physical existence: of animal, plant, and elements, is represented in these GOCs.

In terms of hierarchies of complexity, you could say that the next collective under All That Is might be Entities of various types, representing the collective expression of particular types of humans. The Seth Entity is one example. The human members of this collective are of a particular type. All of us share particular elements of style, behavior, and so on.

Moving on… members of the Seth Entity do prefer to experience all of their lives within Soul Family organizations. This is a case, then, of Seth Entity members, choosing to live lives together. The question may be, here, which of the lives, then, within the Soul Family is an incarnation of Seth. Remember that there are no limitations to consciousness, as I have stated before. It is easier to think of your personality, your consciousness, ending at your skin, for example, than continuing on into your environment and beyond. And so you <u>do</u> limit your perspective, here, so that you may simplify your existence, explain it to yourself in rational terms, and lead a life in your dimension. The truth is much more complex.

An example again: I have also told you that sometimes a particular Soul will experience itself as several family members, and not just one individual. This fact should remind you that the boundaries you see are mental, they do not exist in the truth of your existence.

Back to our book… In this scribe life, it is primarily the Soul Self of Mark who is represented in the life. However, I Seth have participated with him as a fellow student in the monastery and as a mentor, also. I may dip in and out of particular lives to inhabit the human body of these lives. You, Dear Reader, as a "future" Light Body, may also do this. You do it in the dreamstate, for example, where time does not exist. So I hope you see what I am driving at here. Consciousness is fluid. To attempt to pin it down is to attempt to grasp water and hold it.

Spice Merchant

This life of mine, I lived as a hedonist...

Substances

Now we have just today received a request to speak of my life as a spice merchant, and so, even though we have said we would not cover old ground, we will discuss that life briefly that I hinted at in the material created with Jane Roberts and her husband Rob. We will do this as a way to demonstrate how similar Lessons are presented to the Simultaneous Lives, yet each of the lives resolves these Lessons in their own fashion.

Let us be blunt, here, with these descriptions of our - Mark and my - shared lives. There are often issues of addiction in many of the lives of this Entity. Just as is the case with most of you - the humans of the Third Dimension - we have our struggles with appropriate use of substances. So it is, that, in our lives these struggles often appear as Lessons to the experiencing human, though not always. In this life we are discussing, for example, even though there was the taking of powerful snuffs on a regular basis, even though hashish and opium were ingested, even though this fellow suffered the negative realities he helped create through his inappropriate use of substances, he did NOT perceive these experiences and events as Lessons in any way, shape, or form.

Hedonist

This life of mine I lived as a hedonist, a dedicated liver of life "to the nth degree," to use one of our clichés in a humorous way. Mark has used the term "party animal" to describe this personality, but this description is not entirely accurate. A party presumes others are experiencing the life with the subject. The truth is, that this life was lived, for the most part, in relative solitude and loneliness.

I was a successful merchant, a sea merchant specifically, dealing in spices, primarily, including what you might call "contraband" in more modern times. These materials would be marijuana, hashish, opium, and some of the lesser-known African sacraments. I was a connoisseur of these substances as well as an expert on wines, hard liquors, and the spices popular during that era.

The Trade

As a trader in spices I was at sea for most of the year. It was necessary for me to meet with growers and other traders on their turf, in a sense, to make my deals, to discuss business as others would do in less exotic occupations, and so on. I was quite well known to my fellows as a man who could acquire any of the desired substances of the time, in any quantity. The bulk of my profits, indeed, came from these lucrative trades and other deals.

For the most part, these materials were exchanged freely in the open markets. You did not have the drug war that so engages you today. It would not be stretching it too far to suggest that these products were processed with great care and imbibed with great respect and even reverence by myself and by my customers.

Here you see what I am getting at, I hope, with my description of this fellow who does overindulge in his occult "spices," yet does so with an almost sacred perspective guiding him.

Now as I traveled and met with my contacts in the East, I would invariably be introduced to what you would now call "holy men" of various types. All of the sacred substances, it seems, had their various devotees and experts who used the material in a spiritual practice of some sort. These would be called the medicine men, shamans, magicians of the era. During these times, the female practitioner was likely to keep her activities secret, though I was able to supply many of these secretive seekers of the Divine with the sacraments they required. This is a disclaimer, therefore, explaining the absence of the female practitioner in this life. Look to your lives in GA, Dear Reader, for the ascendancy of the female practitioner.

Issues

Now Mark, you have given me permission to discuss your Issues regarding substance use. I will supplement this with what I see as the Issues of my spice merchant. We will cover these private matters in an attempt not to titillate but to inform. ALL of you have issues with these substances including alcohol. Many of you are learning your Primary and Secondary Lessons through your relationships with substances of all kinds. We may even go so far as to include compulsive behaviors such as shopping, sexual behaviors, and others in our analysis here, to show you-the-reader that you are not alone, to coin a phrase. You are, in fact, ALWAYS at the center of a family - a Soul Family - and you are always in all of your lives presented with opportunities to over-indulge, for example, and thus be faced with the after-effects of these behaviors.

Thus, you could say that I was a frequent over-indulger with my substances in this life we are covering here. Long sea voyages were spent, indeed, continually under the influence of substances of one sort or another, including strong alcohol. This was almost a requirement for the seafaring gentleman of that day. Rums and ine-briants of all types were expected to be provided by the captain and others. We who had our own private berths, imbibed alone for the most part, though I would on occasion share and comment on the hashish and sacred snuffs with the captain and his mates. The boredom and monotony of sea travel was thus countered through the consistent use of substances acquired at the various ports.

Once docked within a harbor I would of necessity have to go into the city there to meet with others and procure my goods. It was imperative that I be of clear mental acuity during these times, lest I be taken in a deal not in my favor. This was my social outlet, also, you see, and I did not wish to seem like an out-of-control merchant, one who could not be trusted, and so on. That would not do, and so I played the part of the responsible buyer when in search of my produce. And now a side journey...

Soul Family Gestalt

The Oversoul, or what you may call the Soul Family Gestalt, reflects to the finest delineation of detail, the personality aspects "lived-out" by its multiple existences: the Simultaneous Lives. I have used the term Oversoul at times in my past work with Jane. However, you could also say that this Oversoul is simply the amalgam of creative energies "kept in reserve" by the Soul Family members. From this reserve of potential, each living human draws the requisite definitive energies needed to "fill out" the personality through its experiences in the world. It all happens at once, remember, and so cause-and-effect do not enter here. All of the lives are created whole, all at the same time.

I am attempting to give you the sense of the Soul Family Gestalt as it presents itself eternally, feeding the separate consciousnesses of itself the etheric material needed in any circumstance required. This is all done the better to learn the Lessons of physical existence. And these Lessons are learned consciously or unconsciously - by default, as we say. You may examine my books in The Trilogy for more information on Lessons.

Family Life

Now my family life, for what it is worth. I was a sea-faring trader and so was not what one might call "family man" material. I did have female friends, mates you see, with whom I created children, some 14 children in all during my life. Again, it was expected that the seafarer be away for long periods of time - months and years - and there was not this longing, romantic longing for one another that you see depicted in your movies and other media. This is from my perspective, now. The emotional lives of my various wives were largely unknown to me. It was not that I was uncaring, or callous. I do not believe I was an insensitive person. But it was a condition of that vocation that one would have multiple families stationed at the ports of call. It made things much easier for me. And let us be blunt here, Dear Reader, I chose my wives, in part, for their resiliency and ability to move on with their lives in my absence. We had agreements, therefore, that we would take advantage of one another's company while we may and when I was away, these partners knew that they were completely free to seek out other partners. That is just the state of the matter. There was no guilt and resentment, that I recall. Honesty was the pervading condition in these pairings.

Childhood

My early life in this existence was unremarkable, for the most part. I was a typical boy growing up within a typical small town in what is now Wales. My father was a seafarer and so I decided that I would go to sea also. My mother was not keen on this, however, and resisted my efforts to go aboard ships when my father was in port after a voyage. Father was accustomed to sailing on trade ships around the British Isles, mainly. My wish was to go further, to the European continent and possibly to the Americas, India, and so on. I received some outdated maps of the world as a gift when I was quite young. I studied these maps and became expert on the locations of the countries of the world, the cities within these countries, and the approximate distances between notable destinations on the various trade routes.

Analysis:

As I have said previously, the Seth Entity lives all face challenges of substance use. My life as a spice merchant offered to me an opportunity to learn the Lesson of abstinence and self-control, however, I did not take that opportunity at that time. I reveled in my substance use and created a type of religious practice around it; a hodge-podge of ritual and imagery I learned from my contacts with true holy men and women.

You could say that I renegotiated my life contract in that existence to indulge my appetites freely. However, the Lesson was postponed until a later time, a later incarnation, in your terms. This would be the current lifetime that Mark and I are sharing in your modern world. Now I have told Mark several years ago that I had been "peeking in" on his activities throughout this life. I was well aware of our contract together of meeting-up in this current timeframe and writing books together. I came into his consciousness frequently while he was "in his cups," to coin a phrase. He imbibed alcohol in abundance in his younger years, often to his detriment. On one occasion I spoke with him in Sumari, the language of the non-physical world, and he retained some of that dialogue on awakening. It was only recently, however, that Mark remembered that material and was able to identify it as coming from the Seth Entity.

Mark was not ready in his 30's to begin our project. He re-negotiated his contract to meet with Cas and myself in his 50's. We all agreed on this in the etheric realm to do so. Now I was aware that Mark would be well into his program of abstaining from alcohol when he reached his 50's. I knew that Mark would decide to face this Lesson in his current lifetime. For him, it was a matter of life or death, as his use had reached a critical stage, threatening his relationships, his livelihood, his health. He was highly motivated to NOT deny the Lesson or intellectualize it. He thus faced his Lesson and proceeded to DO THE OPPOSITE of what he had been doing for almost 4 decades. He chose NOT to drink, NOT to deny the spiritual basis of reality, NOT to find reasons for continuing his negative behaviors, you see. As he accepted and began to look for a spiritual basis of reality, I made my move, in a sense, by directing Cas, another member of this Entity, to his hypnotherapy office. All of this was generally known to me well in advance. I am privy to the probable future manifestations of those I peek-in on, and others with whom I have a <u>mutual</u> interest.

I do believe that this case of Mark well represents several of the key concepts I discuss in the new material. You may examine this to prove to yourself what I am saying is true.

Roman Soldier

All civilizations exist contemporaneously...

Dimensions of Time

This life may have been discussed briefly in my work with Ruburt. If you are at all interested you may go back to those texts for corroboration. I do not believe that I have presented material on the Seth Entity existence of the Roman soldier. I offer it to you now. Many of you in my readership have experienced lives as warriors for various collectives. Throughout history, as you understand this term, millions of you, indeed, were pressed into service to defend your territory and even to take the land of others by force. You live in the modern era, and yet look at the correspondences between the practices of the Roman armies and your own armed forces. We are speaking of the U.S., here, but many of the industrialized nations are guilty of creating wars of conquest for the sake of land and the materials on and in that land. I make this disclaimer at this time to remind you that your current existence is created, in a sense, "on top of" these ancient collectives.

Reality Creation

You create your reality in the current moment from your past with your future. Thus, your current modern moment, if you will, contains these archaic seeds of Reality Creation from your perceived past. Let me clarify this for just a moment. *(humorously)* What appears to you-the-reader - the observer of physical reality - as a uniquely modern environment, peopled by modern humans, dressed in modern attire, among the various notable Reality Constructs of modern life - automobiles, electronic devices, jet airplanes - is in fact a complex upgrade or updating of the ancient civilizations, including the Roman Empire. All civilizations exist contemporaneously, in a sort of layered environment, created from the same Consciousness Units that exist throughout eternity.

The Consciousness Units that compose the computer screen in front of you, for example, compose a living tree, or an animal of some kind, or the air itself, in another co-existing civilization from another era in your history or your future. You know this as a reader of my new books and so I shall not pontificate any more than I have to here. I am attempting to demonstrate the "nearness" of this perceived ancient civilization, to you the reader of this book. Your lives, your other lives, my friend, are out there in front of you. They are awaiting your acknowledgement. Therefore, I urge you to consider these possibilities.

Captured

To begin, this life we lived as a soldier in the Roman army was marked by a dedication of service to the Emperor and to the many intermediary officials in the army. I was captured during the sojourns of the mighty Roman armies into what is now Greece. I did not expect anything more than this disciplined servitude to a cause greater than myself.

To be honest, it was a step-up for me, as I merely existed in my life as a teenager, in the olive fields of my family. It was known to all of us in that family that the danger of Roman conquest and enlistment was imminent. One day, I and my older brother were captured by centurions while we were bathing in the river. We were tied on the wrists and put aboard horses to be taken back to the main camp on the outskirts of town. We were told that our parents were given details on why we were taken and the general area of the empire in which we would serve. That day was the last time I would see my parents and sisters.

My brother and I were immediately given rudimentary clothing and gear consisting of leather pleated skirts, metal chest armor, helmets, hand knives and scabbards, and spears. We were designated foot soldiers in the Emperor's army, now, and were promised that we would be allowed to stay in the same collective. However, the next day my brother, who was an excellent wrestler and fighter, and who was almost a full 6 inches taller than I, was taken to work with the horsemen. That was the last time I saw my brother.

I was the child born with the high intellect and the eagerness to read and learn. Because of these natural inclinations, I was allowed to serve as a scribe and attendant to one of the high-ranking officials in the regiment. Thus I was spared from the rigorous training and the dangerous deployments into villages where the soldiers would inevitably meet resistance from farmers, primarily, who might defend to the death their land and their kin.

Dictation

My main duties were to take dictations from my commander and inscribe these messages on paper in ink. I would then read back my notes and add any elaborations this fellow might have, on second thought. Some of these messages entailed secret plans for bringing the forces into Grecian strongholds. This material was treated with the utmost of care and urgency. I was required to take an oath after each of these dictations, to not divulge any of the information to anyone under penalty of death. I took this oath seriously, for it was the breaking of this oath by the scribe previous to me, that lead to his demise. Justice was swift and definite, I can assure you. And there was talk during my tenure that the poor deceased lad was speaking quite innocently to his fellow soldiers when he made his fatal error, perhaps forgetting his oath momentarily.

Obviously I had mixed feelings, being officially a Roman now, when I was ordered not to divulge secret information that villages in my homeland would be attacked. Guilt and other conflicting emotions arose for me on a regular basis. I was a rather skinny and frail boy in this life, and, as I said, I favored the intellect and learning abilities over physical strength.

My Death

I died at the age of 21, bitten by a poisonous snake while sleeping alone in my tent. The snake may have been put in my tent by one of my peers, jealous of the special treatment afforded me by higher-ups. I experienced my Transition from that life with a sense of relief that I would no longer be obligated to participate in the destruction of the villages of my ancestors. As usual, it WAS a surprise that I was still conscious without the physical apparatus. This particular life was not one of enlightenment and seeking out the mysteries of life, in other words. I was a very young Soul with a lot to learn.

Analysis:

This life of the Seth Entity illustrates the importance of what we call "The Scribe Aspect." It is a distinct characteristic of Seth Entity lives, this aspect, that honors the transcribing of spoken or otherwise obtained data *(humorously)* into written form.

Now here we also have a quandary. Is Seth this soldier or is Mark this soldier? It is the same question you might ask about Jane Roberts: Was Jane Seth or was Seth Jane? To answer: I expressed my distinct view of things through Jane and Rob, certainly, as a separate personality essence. She and her husband needed that distinction "for the record," you see, so that they could "believe" and support what was occurring. This served the discussion then, but now I feel it necessary to reveal the true interrelatedness of all consciousnesses within the Seth Entity and within all Oversouls or Entities.

In the case of this soldier, his life was a manifestation of the Seth Entity in physical form. I "remember" my experiences as that human. However, if Mark were to take a voyage in his consciousness, he could also retrieve memories of that life. He is a part of the Seth Entity. Jane was a part. You could also say that all of the Soul Family members of the Jane Roberts collective were members of the Seth Entity, if not directly, by association with other Entities we have called the Families of Consciousness. Consciousness is fluid and pervasive, remember Dear Reader.

Lessons of learning to sustain oneself under servitude to an authoritarian leader were explored in this lifetime. Bleedthroughs from this life to the present, offer Mark "opportunities" to be anxiously oppressed by authority figures in his ongoing life.

Additionally, because he was ruefully remorseful about having to document the plots against his own people, he does experience, at these times of bleedthroughs, a tendency to feel badly about spoiled relationships. It is as though the bleedthroughs remind him of the true value of friendships, family, and so on.

This example was a Young Soul, as we describe it in our books. He took dictation from a power-hungry authority figure. As the Entity grew in knowledge and the experience of Value Fulfillment in numerous other lives, the approach to the Sacred within Earthly life was stressed. The dictation came from non-physical beings of different types. As the Seth Entity "grew" from Young to Old Soul through the incarnations of life, this Scribe Aspect developed. It is as though this aspect of consciousness was inherited by "succeeding" members of the Seth Entity. It is true that the skills necessary for this practice are genetically triggered at the time they are required. I will comment further on this phenomenon at a later time.

Minor Pope

*I spent the entire evening in prayer and writing
about the visitation from Jesus...*

The Church

I have told you before, in works with Jane and her husband, that I once lived a life as a minor Pope. Let me briefly comment on that existence, then, to give breadth to this overview.

I have lived many lives as a dedicated adept of several spiritual paths. The most notable life, however, in so far as notoriety as spiritual practitioner achieved within a single life of the Seth Entity, was as this Pope fellow, a minor Pope in 336 AD.

I was a corrupt leader. Indeed, my path to the office was littered with the destroyed careers of those unlucky enough to get in my way. I was not always such a negative human, however. During a life of privilege, as the son of a wealthy family in what is now central Italy, I was what you might call spoiled, yes, but also certainly of a compassionate and Loving consciousness. Entitled, yes, but also with a deep desire to help others in some way.

Because it was the custom of the wealthy landowners of the time to push for their sons to become priests, I was trained from early on in my life to prepare myself for a life of service to the Catholic Church. The Church was the largest, most powerful, most highly influential "business" in Europe at that time. It was thought by all that a fellow who could maintain a practice as priest for a number of years, could become wealthy and well-respected. It was to this aspect of the priesthood that I responded positively when my father eventually gave me the command to seek training in the local seminary.

Visions at the Seminary

I was a dedicated student at the seminary. The intricacies of the Catholic faith revealed themselves over hours and hours of study and personal tutoring by others. Because I was committed, I was fortunate to experience several awakening events. These visions came to me shortly after instances of prayer and reading of the sacred scripts. In the most powerful vision I was approached by Jesus himself who asked for my dedicated service to the work at hand. He did not speak words; it was a mental transmission that I read within his eyes as he looked down upon me from his position, elevated to several feet in the air above me. Within the confines of my little room, the vision shimmered and pulsated, somewhat like a nocturnal dream. Here my eyes were indeed wide open. My senses were acute and ready for the communication, whatever it might be. I felt deeply humbled to have the object of my affections and religious studies pay me a visit personally. I was so over-whelmingly pleased, yet startled by the presentation, that I could not speak coherently. I believe that I did, however, thank him mentally.

I asked that he assist me along the way to the priesthood, also, if I am not mistaken. Then, in a moment, the vision faded to the darkness of my room in the night. I could not sleep after that and so I spent the entire evening in prayer and writing about the visitation from Jesus.

When I told my teachers about the event on the next morning, most of them took it quite seriously and enthusiastically, as a sign, as a good sign for my future development. Unfortunately for me, however - at least I thought it unfortunate at the time - my study and prayer curriculum was intensified and lengthened beginning the next day.

I was a quick learner and I moved forward rapidly in my studies at the seminary. Spurred on by donations of great wealth from my family, the church leaders saw fit to move me quite ahead of the others, into a position as assistant to a priest in the town of Elna. I was delighted to be on my own, somewhat. Finally away from both family and church authorities, it seemed as though I was indeed destined for greatness, just as my father had stated numerous times to me in my youth. At that time, however, I assumed he was referring to my taking over the reins of the family business. Now I know that he also had other plans for me of a more etheric nature.

To the Vatican

Again, through the behind-the-scenes manipulations, proddings, and gift benefits of my family, I was allowed to take over the priestly duties in the little church, allowing my colleague Father Ginis to go to another more prosperous diocese in the North of Italy. Immediately, then, under the intimate guidance of my father and some local business men, I began to amass my fortune.

At the time, it was thought by the general population of church-going humans, that one could buy oneself an improved station in the afterlife, by contributing to the local church. With this in mind, the wealthy and not-so-wealthy of the diocese were encouraged to give as much as they could afford, and more, to the church. A percentage of this income was sent to Rome, a percentage was kept to fund the operation of the church, some was given to the poor and kept for other charitable enterprises, and a small percentage was taken by the priest. This small percentage, however, quickly grew to a small fortune. The other churches and their leaders were all keenly aware of how much each priest would accrue in this process. The power and substance of individual priests was, then, determined by this amassing of wealth. The value of the diocese was determined by this amalgam of contributed wealth and property. And the wealthier the diocese, the higher the standing within the church hierarchy of the church leader.

To make a long story short - I promised to be brief here - I quite quickly became noted for my business sense, for my perceived reverence, for my connections to wealthy business men, and so found myself on the fast track to the Vatican.

Elected Cardinal

Having served a short time, compared to others, I was elected to the position of Cardinal and then Pope. My stay in the Vatican as Pope was very brief. I delegated most of my duties to others and was pleased to be allowed to drink my wine and attend to my prayers and study. I enjoyed my private time and did not blend well with the pomp and ceremony of the papal office. When it was all over, I was relieved to surrender the office to another. I was not meant for this type of leadership position. I was a scribe and a seeker of visions. The last year of my life was spent in the pursuit of solitude and peace.

The Alexander Projection

Mark: Seth, at one time you said to me in one of our sessions that the date was 1200 AD and you suggested the Pope was named Alexander. There was an Alexander IV in the 1200's. Is this the Pope you were speaking of at that time?

Seth: Look it up on your internet Mark.

(I did and discovered Seth originally said 300+ AD in the old material. There was a Pope in 336; St. Marcus or St. Mark.)

Mark: Seth, can we talk a bit about the validity of this material?

Seth: Yes, a moment Mark. The question of validity will always arise. It is the nature of the beast, you see. It is a necessary part of our relationship, this continually proving the validity of the material to yourself. I realize that it is not enough for you to have faith in our work together, even though, if you were to do so, it would smooth out this process greatly. The validity of the material is determined by a number of factors, the primary one being your depth of trance and the solidity of the connection to the Seth Entity. You will get imprecise information when you are not in direct contact.

For the record, the date is 336 for the Pope. It is Pope Mark. The comparisons are obvious between yourself, another Mark, and this Pope. You can sense your connection if you would care to guide yourself to that life.

The 1200 date was a reference to another connection of mine to the Pope of that time, Alexander. This you picked up quite clearly. You may use this if you wish, or not. However, I was able to briefly experience some ongoing elements of his life as Pope. I projected an aspect of my experiencing Soul Self into his consciousness. He was not aware of it, to a large degree, though he did experience an elevation of perception when I engaged his consciousness in this way. To this human, it seemed as though the Divine was making an appearance. Is this helping you?

Mark: Yes. I'm wondering why you haven't mentioned this in your older works with Jane?

Seth: There was no need to mention it, Mark. I only mentioned the 336 Papal existence in passing. If someone were to ask, I would have divulged information on this projection, however, this was not the case. I am sorry if you are confused. My advice is to move through the autobiography quickly, complete it and move on with our other projects. Please work toward a deep trance state for our communications. These doubts will be resolved when you deepen the connection. Will that be all?

Mark: Yes Seth. Thanks

Seth: You are welcome. Good morning and good luck. *(humorously)*

Analysis:

What shall we make of this life and this projection of consciousness? The aspects of the visionary are evident here. The members of this Entity are often predisposed to looking for the deeper meanings of life, through spiritual practice, most notably.

There is this seeking of wealth, also, that stands in the background, highlighting all of the endeavors of the life. The Scribe Aspect is noted, as well as this tendency for solitude, solitary practice, you see.

Now the projection of consciousness to the life of Alexander, almost a millennium after the life of Pope Mark, holds other data. This Alexander was much more active and a great deal more productive than Mark. I was interested, therefore, to see the differences, here, between what I experienced as a passive, disinterested Pope and what this Alexander experienced as an enthused, confident, and empowered Pope. The differences I see are largely attributable to physical health matters. Mark was sickly, Alexander robust and vital. Mark was a loner with a penchant for wine. Alexander was a gregarious type, eager to work with his staff to implement changes in the church of Rome to consolidate power. These activities took place within the pomp and ceremony that Mark despised. Alexander used wine ceremoniously, not as a drug, as did Mark. Thus you could say that these two examples show the two sides of the same coin that is the typical Seth Entity human enjoying physical existence. I will allow the reader to make those comparisons.

Let me also, if I may, comment on a subject we covered in our book on Soul Family. This would be the tendency for the explorer of Reincarnational Lives to visit lives of note, of glamour, of celebrity. This is quite common for all explorers of consciousness, including, obviously, Seth. I do this, however, to draw the reader into the conversation for effect. When you go on your own excursions to your lives, you will possibly discover some that are of note. This may make the process fun and quite enjoyable for you, and if that is the case, excellent. The exploration of the psyche and the multidimensional self SHOULD be pleasurable. To be sure, as you reach a comprehensive understanding of your greater creaturehood in these explorations, you may well find that pleasure, ecstasy, pleasant feelings, fill your consciousness. This is a pleasant by-product of seeking out the Divine. It is quite normal, Dear Reader.

Italian Woman

She is in Love, you see...

Correspondences

Mark: Would you like to work on the Italian female life? Or anything else is OK with me.

Seth: Yes Mark. Please notice how, in this pleasant setting, as you look across your beautiful lake at the volcano on the other side, it is quite easy to sense this spacious moment in time. I am bringing you deeper for this transmission...

There are correspondences between these lives of ours, that are noticed within this spacious moment - a Moment Point, if you will. Then, even as you are now marveling at the beauty of the picturesque scene before you, you and I, our other life is also experiencing a pleasurable moment in time. This young woman of Italian descent is enjoying the view at a beach in Southern Italy. There she is smiling at a pair of ducks as they waddle by, just as you

Mark, smiled at the ducks walking past your picnic table. These correspondences you share, then, are composed of emotion, inner imagery, Feeling-Tones, you see. Let us move on in our description.

Good Humor

This female life of ours from the 1600's is experiencing satisfaction - what we would call a Good Humor moment in our books. She is in Love, you see; romantically attracted to a fellow who lives and works in this coastal village. Leana is, however, of a lesser social status than this young man, who is the heir to the estate, which includes beach property, houses, farmland, and so on. Leana's family has far less in the way of an estate. She has been forbidden to associate with this man. They grew up together, in the sense that her parents did some work for the boy's family over the years. This work had to do with woodworking and the skills necessary to maintain gardens and vineyards.

This description is of simply one moment in time. The emotional tone, the Feeling-Tone, you see, is one of satisfaction, generally, but with this shadow of melancholy. It is as though the good feelings of momentary ecstasy could not be appreciated WITHOUT this low-grade sadness; sadness for impending loss, let us say.

Analysis:

Now in my analysis, here, this Feeling-Tone I have just described is used quite often by the Seth Entity - by the lives of the Seth Entity - to create moments of Reality Creation that stand as the physical results of the Feeling-Tone. It is as though there is a difficulty completely surrendering to the dearness and intimacy of the moment. The fear of future lack - in this case, of the future absence of the beloved - effectively prevents complete absorption in the moment of ecstasy. The restriction of emotion creates a reality for the Soul Self of less-than-complete Loving surrender.

Feeling-Tone

Remember that all of our lives, all of your lives, Dear Reader, are holographically connected. When one of the Simultaneous Lives experiences a particular Feeling-Tone in the moment, BECAUSE you are connected to all of your lives, you and all of your lives are immediately affected. Yes, immediately and spontaneously within the spacious moment, to continue the metaphor, all lives are changed to the atomic level. Thus we may say that you-the-reader exist as the momentary culmination of the reciprocal Reality Creation energies of all of your

Simultaneous Lives. In the next moment, you-the-reader are altered again, according to the momentary Feeling-Tones experienced by all of your lives, and so on.

Options

Now: The plot thickens here in our romance. Our heroine Leana is about to act out of character and our friend Mark is inspired by these messages. He is noticing the self-limiting Feeling-Tone within his consciousness. He is entertaining a desire to move out of that self-limiting Feeling-Tone and expand his beliefs. He is experiencing an epiphany, of sorts, and is opening up to new probabilities of cultivating ecstasy, surrendering in the moment to Love, etc.

Also, within this moment, our Leana is opening up to improved probabilities, probable futures that include the beloved young man in her existence. She is changing her consciousness, surrendering to Love, imagining a probable future existence WITH the beloved, despite the disapproval of her family.

So these are two examples, here. However, all of the lives of the Seth Entity are experiencing within this spacious moment, an awakening according to the specifics of their individual personalities, their individual belief systems, and emotional bodies.

Bisexuality of the Psyche

Let me briefly comment on an issue that has just now crossed my mind. It pertains to the intrinsic bi-sexuality of the psyche or Soul Self. In this example, our Lover is longing to go outside the boundaries of societal acceptance and proclaim her Love for the boy from the rich family. In other lives of this Seth Entity, however, there are at the same moment, males who are longing to do precisely this same thing with other males and females with other females.

It is the same all-consuming Love that drives the behaviors of all of these participants in physical reality. The same goes for the lives being lived by you-the-reader. This Love with a capital L we speak of in the books is felt by both men and women in the same way. This powerful emotion transforms both men and women in the same way. The reactions of both men and women to the power of Love, by surrendering to Love, for example, are the same.

Therefore, given this bi-sexuality of the psyche, I dispute any notions that women feel love differently than men, or that men are coldly calculating in

Love and women are not. In truth, Love transforms everyone, man and woman alike, once you have surrendered to its power.

French Colonial Period
Female of High Estate

The wife was a reluctant participant...

Entitlement

This life is related to the Fragment Existence we shall cover in the next chapter. You will understand this statement when you have read both chapters.

Now we refer to this life of the Seth Entity as one of High Estate. This was the term used in that era, during the French Colonial Period in what is now known as Louisiana, to refer to someone of entitlement, inherited wealth.

This woman came to the New World of North America with her husband, a wealthy merchant. He found success selling items useful to the settlers: furs, tools, and so on. The husband was a trader who developed his fortune in

France, and then, being of an adventurous mind, traveled to North America and set up his business in the port cities of Louisiana, near the Mississippi delta.

The wife was a reluctant participant in this adventurous quest. The woman quite enjoyed her refined life that she lived in France, on the Southern coast of that country. She felt that she was to live out her existence as a wealthy heiress, after the husband had passed on. This was not to be the case, however, and it was with great anguish and screaming that she accompanied her husband to the delta region.

Embodiment

You may have noticed how I keep a type of distance between myself and my descriptions of some of these Seth lives. This is a case in point, here, and I shall tell you why I am doing so. It is because I was not completely embodied within the consciousness of this female. Yes, these are the lives of the Seth Entity. Yet some are lived in varying degrees of embodiment and investment, you might say.

To be blunt: the main Lesson I was to learn here was one of acknowledging the entitlement and paucity of values - the human virtues, you see - within my consciousness. And then, the task was to address these deficits and remove or reverse them. Please note how this illustrates the abilities of the Soul Self. Even as the Soul - the

Oversoul if you wish - cooperates with and feeds energy to countless fully-embodied existences all at the same "time," we may also dip in an out of these other less-embodied lives to learn our Lessons and to participate with Soul Family members there.

To return... this is a story of a Soul experiencing the challenges of, not only traveling great distances to begin an entirely new life on a distant continent, but to also be engaged in a deep and transformative, soul-searching enterprise.

Tragedy

Now the merchant gentleman set up his store immediately on moving to the Mississippi area of North America. He became quite successful within a few months time, as he was able to offer, again, just as he had done in his native land, those goods and services that people actually desired. The wife, our challenged life, you see, was at least for the time being, satisfied with her lot, and helped her husband to set up his shop and to oversee the day-to-day activities there. Unfortunately for this life of ours, her husband was killed a few months into the new venture, when he was trampled by a team of horses in the streets in front of his business. This tragedy, again, as tragedies so often do, served to spin our life off onto a different mode of living and of Reality Creation.

This was her/our primary Lesson that was unfolding. It was a Lesson of lessening the ego/intellect, surrendering the feelings of pomposity and greed, and learning about how to survive on one's own, using one's wits and natural abilities.

Success

This woman did succeed in carrying on the activities of the shop and she did so in a very exemplary fashion, in so far as, she WAS a woman doing what was thought of as a man's job in the early formative years of the United States. She did succeed and she did maintain her husband's connections to the European and Eastern U.S. traders. She kept alive those trading routes that allowed her to continue to supply the peoples in her territory with the goods and services they required.

Also, though she was inclined to be less than demonstrative and active in sexual matters with her husband, after his death she "bloomed," and took on a series of lovers. This turnaround had the effect of further empowering this life of ours, to the degree that she was asked to run for a leadership position in the city. She declined and instead took on a permanent mate and bore two children in her 30's.

She retired at the age of 41, allowing her trained staff to run the store, which by that time had grown to be the largest of its type in the territory. This life of ours made her transition at the age of 46, due to an internal infection that was not treated in time.

Analysis:

This life is one in which the Feeling-Tone of prosperity and a perception of the Abundant Universe, as we say in our books, was exemplified. You could say that in this life we came full-circle in our understanding, our understanding as a Soul. Humility was quite absent in the beginning of this life. Born into a wealthy family, engaged to a promising businessman at an early age, all of the wants and needs were satisfied for this human at all times. The feelings of being entitled to the privileged life were what were to be met with the discerning eyes of the Soul Self, and then countered in physical reality through a Reincarnational Drama of convincing power. Thus the turnaround with the death of the mate and the necessity to fend for oneself.

Now along with the attending to the running of the business by this self of ours, came the realization that there was what one might call a "blessing" in the perceived hardship of having to take on the business chores. This was precisely the opposite of what the woman expected. She did not expect to be introduced to her own power through the loss of the husband. And as she trudged forward she felt humility dawning within her consciousness. She became overwhelmed with gratitude to her vague notion of what God is, for allowing her to survive and prosper in this new land.

Let us also look at the Feeling-Tone of prosperity that bleeds through into the current existence of my friend Mark, here, to influence his consciousness. The Feeling-Tone within the mental environment of this woman was impressive, for it was born out of suffering and the necessity to take on the task of the husband's business. She truly was required to dig deep, here, and summon up the motivation and inner resources to succeed. When she did succeed and was able to relax a bit, you might say, the gratitude comes through for her. Humility, gratitude, faith in a positive outcome, all of these delicate hues color this Feeling-Tone of accomplishment, of abundance.

I trust I am not being too obscure here. I am attempting to get through to my colleague Mark to direct his attention to this Feeling-Tone that can empower him and his activities in this project. This Feeling-Tone is ALWAYS there to inspire and to nurture. All of you have similar bleedthroughs, as you encounter the potential to be inspired by your other lives.

Current Personality Fragment

She escaped the devastation of Katrina...

(In this section, I asked Seth to clarify for the reader an event in which, apparently, I subconsciously projected a fragment of my consciousness into a mother-to-be in Louisiana. mf)

On a Mission
Mark: Seth, you have already told me something about this fragment of consciousness. My main question now is this: "Is the mother still alive?"

Seth: Yes the Mother is still alive. She escaped the devastation of Katrina and the collapsing levees. She moved to New Mexico before these tragedies occurred. Now let us recap what has gone before between us, Mark, for the edification of the reader. A moment...

From your Moment Point, in a time and place in the past, during the 90's, as you may remember, you projected a fragment of your consciousness. You might say that this aspect of your consciousness was on a "mission," a mission to the past, several decades, now, to effect and motivate the consciousness of a female living in New Orleans. You facilitated the consciousness of this woman with accepting a proposal from a man to become pregnant and carry a child that would be given to the man at birth. In a sense, you could say that you inspired this female to go through with the project with positive emotions, Love, as we call it in the books: Love with a capital L. During the pregnancy of this woman, she was inspired, by you personally, Mark, to move forward with Love, with an expectation of a positive future for herself and the child.

Collaborative Effort

Now this is the projection phenomenon. In this case, it is a collaborative effort between Soul Family members. Your Oversoul, Mark, created the necessary connections in the non-physical world to make this happen. It was a subconscious manifestation, for the most part. Now that you have become aware of it in the last few years, you are participating consciously. However, when you met the child as an adult, you were quite unaware of these connections. You only knew that you were attracted to this person as a friend and colleague, for you shared the same love for service to the underprivileged, to the poor.

Mothering

To clear this up somewhat, you sent this fragment out subconsciously several years before you were to meet this adult human female. You were setting the stage for meeting her, and for providing emotional support for her while she was in need of support. You cared for her as a mother or loving father would care for a person. This stems from that initial collaboration with the birth mother, you see.

Seth: Mark, you may delete those parts of this narrative that you feel might be too personal. But please leave enough information to allow the material to be understood by the average reader.

Mark: OK Seth.

Seth: Again, ALL OF YOU are experts at this projection activity. This is one way that you participate with others in the learning of Lessons. Most of the creative process occurs in the dreamstate, within your collective unconsciousness, where you are connected to everyone generally and your Soul Family members specifically.

Collective Unconscious

If you can imagine, again, this powerful computer of the collective unconscious that plans, strategizes, and then implements these programs for meeting up with members of your Soul Family throughout time. It is as though, because you have enough to do in physical reality, just to keep moving forward in your existence, all of the connections are made for you automatically, spontaneously, in the so-called unconscious states.

The Shift

This brings us to the Shift in Consciousness that is occurring for all of you in your system. As the Shift unfolds, each of you becomes more and more aware of your greater existence, what we call the Simultaneous Lives, the Unknown Reality, and so on. As you, as an awakening human, become accustomed to holding within your consciousness the data you are receiving from these other lives, you will also regain awareness of projections of consciousness, such as the one I am describing now.

Computer

To use the computer comparison once again... it will be as though you will be utilizing a completely new and efficient interface on the computer of your existence. The inner workings of your Reality Creation will be made known to you, appearing on the computer screen of your perceptions. Naturally, this will take some getting used to. Multitasking, we call it. You will become quite adept at interacting with your other lives, while you, at the same time, now, carry on with the mundane duties and behaviors of your current existence in your current timeframe.

Analysis:

What was learned by the Entity and by Mark and others in this projection of consciousness? Certainly the value of Love was fulfilled; a type of non-romantic Love, you see. This relationship that grew from the projection proved to the participants that men can be motherly towards others and that it can be appreciated as such. Your roles that you fulfill in reality are often limited by your culture's insistence on keeping the expression of your Loving between certain boundaries. It is good to break through these boundaries and not limit yourself to your societal role.

Indeed, it has been my suggestion in the new books, that the average citizen of your planet could just as easily express Loving Understanding for ANYONE they happen to meet. Anyone, including strangers, you see, may be assessed with Loving Understanding and Courage.

One other important Lesson learned here is the obvious one of the phenomenon of projection itself. Mark was initially astounded when I told him what he had done in this instance of Reality Creation. He was incredulous until I described the specific process by which he co-created the "coincidental" meeting with the human in question.

It explains quite a bit, this projection phenomenon. The reader may look for instances of this phenomenon within their own Reality Creation. If you are diligent, you will find your own examples.

Atlantean Life

*I was primarily an educator
in this existence...*

Your Intent

Now at the risk of alienating our "scientists" in the reading audience, I believe we shall cover the Atlantean existence. First this preface, however, in an attempt to make the information palatable and understood to those of you who prefer the histories of your media. I have stated before this fact of your existence: all events occur all of the time. Everything, in other words, that has the potential to exist, does indeed exist. This is true for everyone and everything in your world. It is an absolute: a truth of your system.

Further, to embrace this truth, rather than find something wrong with it, sets you up for an experiencing of this moment in which All That Is creates everything there is to create. You create your own reality. If you have doubts about the veracity of a particular statement of mine, or of anyone else, you blind yourself to that reality. However, if you keep a very open mind here, by postponing your disbelief, you may entertain the possibility of Mystery Civilizations, spirit phenomena, and so on.

Will you then, if you are rather skeptical of this information on Atlantis, hear me out? Turn off the censor of the ego/intellect for just a few moments, my friend.

Now ALL civilizations conceived by the human collective on Earth and elsewhere exist here and now. It all happens at once. Everything in created reality exists there before you, regardless of where you are, regardless of what time it is, regardless, even, of your incredulity that such a thing is possible. It is all happening now, Dear Reader. The Atlantean civilization is in its fruition, you might say, now in this moment, just as it is ALWAYS in fruition at all moments.

This leads us to a technique the student may use in accessing the Simultaneous Lives. On the assumption that what I say is true, that everything exists at once, in completion, so to speak, you may think of yourself as homing-in on those lives at the specific point in which there is this mutual learning of Lessons. Therefore, assuming you have lived a life in the Atlantean times, you would consider, in the Trance state, at what point within this life you could travel to receive information that would benefit your life in this modern timeframe. Your Intent serves as the guidance system here. Your focus on what may exist that is of benefit to you, in a wondering type of exercise, you see, opens you up to the possibilities of looking into these lives, to see where you may gain some insight.

The Life

Now that you are in the proper mind-set to experience this other reality, let me briefly relate a few facts of this Atlantean existence.

This life of ours, Mark, was notable for the accumulation of power and knowledge during the lifetime. I was primarily an educator in this existence, a male. The education system of this culture was as described in *Mystery Civilizations*. Lessons of all types were learned in the waking AND dreaming states. The Ancient Wisdom, as we have referred to it in the new books, was imparted to students of all ages through telepathic transmissions. It was my responsibility to transmit telepathically the information to the sleeping consciousnesses of students. On awakening, we would have follow-up sessions in classrooms in Third-Dimensional Reality.

Now: as well as teaching, I was obliged to lend my talents to various collectives within the community. I helped in a planning agency, for example. Those of us who had a knack for perceiving future events, were enlisted to make suggestions on building development, water systems, communication networks, and so on. We were innovators and seers in this capacity and we served our community without pay, but certainly, through trading our services for other goods and services that we required to live. There was no currency, per se, merely this trade and barter system that saw that everyone was taken care of, and that all were allowed to use their talents for the greater good.

The Practice

As for the accumulation of power in this life, we were honored and rewarded to the degree that we could accurately predict what would occur within consensus reality during a given time period. I was quite skilled at this practice, and so I did garner rewards, vouchers for goods and services from the community, and so on.

I married during this life at an advanced age: I was in my 60's before I took a mate for the first time. I fathered 6 children with that woman. We were in Love, this is true, however we were primarily partners in the exploration of the physical and non-physical worlds. We were scientists, and we worked as a team, engaged in a continuous effort to remember the Ancient Wisdom and apply these principles in our lives, to help, to heal, to create happiness within our family and within the families of others who would come to us for assistance.

This practice of healing saw my partner and I exploring the uses of sound and light to relieve maladies of various types. We were quite successful with what you might call the "emotion-generated" illnesses. These would be anxiety disorders, as you now call them, and the psychosomatic conditions. These practices, fueled by our interest in the human mind and in the creation of reality itself from consciousness, would be enjoyed by many other Seth Entity lives in "future" incarnations. You could say that this is a definite tendency of this Entity, to attempt to look within the psyche, to assess, and to attempt to bring balance, a balance of consciousness.

Light and Sound

There was a tradition in our healing practice at that time to make use of light and sound techniques to assist our clients in attaining and keeping a meditative state, one you might call a Trance state. Crystals and gems of different types, including quartz, amethyst, ruby and others, were used as lenses to carry the sun's light and the moon's light and to transmit and focus these spectrums upon the patient who was seeking healing. Music, primarily flute and chime sounds, bells, gongs and other instruments were used to invoke specific states of consciousness.

The sound of flowing water was used to help the client relax and go within. These techniques were developed over generations of experimentation by practitioners in our family.

Thus, the healing chamber, as I knew it then, was a small arena or stage, on which the client would be seated or laid down in the center. The musicians, the light machine operators, and the chanting attendants surrounded this client and engaged in a precise enactment or dramatization of healing myths from our histories. In this way the Ancient Wisdom was imparted to those in need of healing. They were reminded that they are the creators of their world, including their physical bodies. The healing rituals specific to the malady in question were enacted to create a quite impressive and memorable healing experience. Dramatic spontaneous healings were expected and occurred quite frequently in these sessions.

Analysis:

Now what was learned in this life... primarily the Ancient Wisdom was remembered and practiced with regards to prophecy and healing. First let me remind you, all of you at some point in your Simultaneous Lives are practitioners of magic, healers, prophets, and so on. Many of you, indeed, tend to incarnate to live lives as these magicians, shamans, witches and healers we speak of in the books. In this case, Mark and I explored prophecy and healing as a vocation. I was the male here, the husband of Mark the female. Other members of Mark's Soul Family throughout time show up here in this distant life also, in different bodies to learn their Lessons with us. The Lessons of awakening together were explored, here, as Mark and I dedicated our very lives to scientific investigation of the Unknown Reality.

Spontaneous Healing

The concept of Spontaneous Healing we explored in the lab that was our healing arena. Both of us were guided by the communication stream of the Ancient Wisdom. This is true. However, we also were privy to "future" discoveries, scientific discoveries that would not occur, in your terms, for many thousands of years. We used the information gained from sojourns into our distant past and to your inconceivably distant future to learn the skills necessary, and to be "initiated" into forms of practice that would allow us to be successful in our healing approach. We reached back into our histories as Star Beings, before even our journey to Earth to establish the human species. We also, as I said, visited quite distant futures on Earth, tens of thousands of years in your future, when the Star People return to their ancestral home.

Prophecy and healing... these were stressed, then, even as these talents and tendencies are stressed now by this Seth Entity in the life of Mark. I hope I am inspiring you-the-reader to wonder about your possible Star origins. Wondering is where it begins.

Animal Fragments

*The distinctions between species become blurred
during these moments...*

Projections of Consciousness

I feel that it would be appropriate to speak of this
practice of projecting a fragment of consciousness, of
Soul you might also say, into animals and other non-human
creatures. I spoke of this briefly in my work with
Jane Roberts, Ruburt. Here let me again normalize this
by assuring the reader that any one of you with practice
can accomplish this projection of consciousness. It has
been perfected by your visionaries over the generations,
by your native peoples who practice shamanism, by nature poets and others who intensely use their Intention to
experience Earthly existence from within the consciousness of other inhabitants of the natural world.

The Basics

Getting back to the basics, here, in my theory of manifestation. You ARE connected to everything via the Consciousness Units. *(See Glossary. mf)* And thus you have a kinship, not only with the animals in your world, but also, unbelievably, with every other Reality Construct in your reality. Knowing this, do you see how easy it is to create an affinity of consciousness with any animal in your world? You do this quite often when you have a pet that you identify with and Love unconditionally. The distinctions between species become blurred during these moments...

Now at this time I am not inhabiting a physical body, per se, however it is quite easy for me to project a fragment of my experiencing consciousness into animals in the 3rd Dimension, so that I may once again experience the Earth from the perspective of the animal. I am borrowing the animal's perceptive faculties when I project myself in this way. Here let me just say that I still keep in touch with the 3rd Dimension through these practices. As Mark can tell you, he often senses my presence through his beloved animals, and validates these perceptive breakthroughs.

Post-Transition
Environments

*It is an etheric body that you
have at your disposal...*

The Home Dimension

Now: somewhat as an introduction to the material we shall cover in a forthcoming book on Death and the Afterlife, let me speak a bit on the consciousness of the Third-Dimensional human that occurs, if you will, AFTER the death of the physical form. As you know, your physical death marks the beginning of other deep and meaningful existences within other dimensions. The Home Dimension is the one I would like to cover now. This dimension of experiencing the personal consciousness of the human individual, lies outside of time and of space. The Home Dimension holds, quite literally, the individual private existences of the Seth Entity, and indeed, of ALL of you in physical reality, that occur outside of the physical body, in the non-physical world.

So your private consciousness expression - your particular personality, holding within it the memories of experiences lived within your time on Earth - survives the Transition: the death of corporeal form. Please try to imagine this concept of the eternal existence of the private consciousness. It exists in a sort of electromagnetic environment that sustains all Transitioned Souls. Your quaint descriptions of Heaven and the Afterlife come into play here. Those of you who have had near death experiences, and have retained memories of those experiences, know what I am saying here.

Etheric Body

Briefly, this state of consciousness is quite pleasant to behold. For the newly deceased, for example, you are usually experiencing this world from within an etheric counterpart to your physical body construct, to the body you used in the prior incarnation, in other words. It is an etheric body that you have at your disposal to explore the post-transition environments and the Earthly environments you have just left.

It is through this vehicle of perception that you experience a replay of your life in the physical dimension. You note the high points and the low. You examine where

Lessons were learned, avoided, or postponed. You may call up, as on a great holographic computer display, any event from your life or lives, for examination, for scrutiny, you see. It is this interactive communication with the Third-Dimension that creates opportunities for so-called "spirit phenomena." Sensitive humans from their Soul Family who are still in the physical body may sense their activities. Also, sensitives generally are quite able to sense the goings-on of the Transitioned human explorers of the physical world. The Transitioned human is simply re-experiencing the physical world.

Ghosts

Obviously, here, we are explaining to you the facts of life with regards to ghosts. Again, there is no need to fear your so-called ghosts. It is true, that, on occasion, a Transitioned Human Soul will become confused and not find their way out of the physical dimension of 3D Reality. They may cause some discomfort for those they contact. Let me just say that if you can manage to create the OPPOSITE of fear: Loving Understanding, here, on these rare occasions of contact, this will help both of you. Gently direct the lost Soul to the Home Dimension. Use the Telepathic Network to Lovingly direct them away from the Third Dimension and to the realm of the ancestors. This will help you also, for you will have gained some experience communicating with a Transitioned Soul, and you will not be completely naive when the time comes for your own Transition.

Analysis:

What has the Seth Entity learned from these respites in the Home Dimension? The gratitude for having lived lives on Earth is overwhelming to the newly Transitioned Soul. The cliche that you do not know the importance or dearness of something until you have lost it, applies here. This is particularly true when I have made a Transition from a life as a Young Soul.

I have made many journeys into Earthly life as a young, careless spirit, and have caused much pain to those with whom I came in contact. I have discovered, that, moments after death, the true treasure that is a human life comes into sharp focus. As hurtful moments in time come into view in the holographic recall, the intensity of shame and the feeling of lost opportunity create a truly teachable moment for the Soul. You make a vow to do things differently next time. And then you plunge ahead into another life.

The Dimension
of Virtue

*Fear and anger and the other negative emotions
are not allowed here...*

Gestalts of Consciousness

There is a dimension, a state of consciousness that
I visit quite often, solely for the peace, comfort, and
Loving sustenance that I experience there. In fact, I spend
so much time in this environment that you could say it is
a life of mine that I am enjoying there. The Dimension of
Virtue is simply the repository of the virtuous emotions,
thoughts, and imagery of humanity.

Over time, your thoughts have effects. They assemble, as you know, into Gestalts of Consciousness that act
as the blueprints for reality as All That Is creates all that
may be created. The truism that, "Every good thought
has a positive effect," comes in here. It is true, that all
thoughts, negative or positive, seek out expression in

terms of Value Fulfillment. However, I am not speaking of Heaven, here. Humanity's ideas of pleasant afterlifes are real, in the sense that, everything that may be imagined is real. Yet this Dimension of Virtue is a specific and quite "generic" expression of "all that is good" in human thought, emotion, behavior, imagery, and so on.

When I visit this state I am immediately reminded of the truth of our existence: that all is Love. When you are surrounded by this Loving imagery, ideation, and emotion, it does fill your senses. Fear and anger and the other negative emotions are not allowed here, obviously. The negative emotions have their dimensions in which they play out, in which they "inspire" the propagators of negative realities.

The Dimension of Virtue is the inspiration for doing good works, just for the sake of doing good works. It is the state of consciousness that fuels the expression of all of the virtues in the Third Dimension. It is the "vacation destination," in a manner of speaking, for Transitioned Souls who wish to "recharge their batteries," before moving into another physical life on Earth.

Your Multidimensional Autobiography

*You continue on this path until you reach
Light Body status...*

Your Story

We have come to the end of our survey of some lives of
this Seth Entity. We have purposely led you through his-
torical lives in the Third Dimension and to the ephemeral
existences within the non-physical world. This is the cy-
cle, you see. You are always returning to the non-physical world for rest, for reflection, for strategizing. Then,
for most of you, the journey requires another experience
of the physical. You continue on this path until you reach
Light Body status and then you may retire, you might
say, to a "life" of study, experimentation, observation,
such as I have chosen.

Your Multidimensional Existence

In this final message to you, I would ask you to examine YOUR multidimensional existence. Where are you on your Soul's path? How many and what types of lives have you lived and are you living? This analysis is done with the activated imagination. You simply achieve a meditative state, tuning into your Source, your Guidance, your Intuition.

You would then direct a line of inquiry to your Guidance, as to what lives of yours are the most accessible in this light Trance. It is as though you have some lives that are "favorites" of yours, in that, you favor going to them in the dreamstate, and in times of reverie, for purposes of gathering information or receiving inspiration. Obviously, you "forget" this material instantaneously. At the moment of capture and processing, you forget.

Interviews

In this exercise, you will be attempting to keep these memories in the conscious mind. Give yourself the suggestion, before entering your Trance State, that you will have full memories of what transpires during the session. Have some questions memorized that you wish to ask these other lives. Interview these characters telepathically when you make contact.

Now you will know that you have made contact when you get a strong emotional "hit" during the session. It is a good feeling to make contact with another reincarnational life. This is the "elementary ecstasy" we speak of in our books. Your activated imagination will then pick up this thread of contact and communication and see where it leads. A narrative may develop. Images of the other existence may flash on the inward eye. Aromas and tactile sensations are common. All of this information you will remember after you give yourself the suggestion to come out of your Guided Meditation with "all data intact and ready for transcription."

Timing

Let me make this important point regarding timing in contacting your other lives. The question may arise for you: "Why do I meet my other lives at various ages of their lives? Is there a connection to my current age here in this existence?" Let me clarify that if I may.

As I said before, you favor collaborating with particular lives at particular stages of THEIR development, at particular times in YOUR development. Therefore, when you meet a life at a time in their youth, let us say, you can be sure that you are currently, in your modern timeframe, relying on the information within the consciousness of this youthful existence to create your own reality. You are both considering similar Issues, in other words. You are both learning similar Lessons. Later in your current existence, you may find it helpful to access this other target existence at an elderly stage of development. It is up to you.

A Touchstone

It was my main concern in this manuscript to compare and contrast the essences of personality of these Simultaneous Existences of the Seth Entity. I was not as thorough, therefore, as some would like. We are providing this material for the reader to use as a touchstone to guide them into an exploration of their own multi-dimensional, multi-existence experiencing. This is another windy disclaimer to remind you that the work is before you, Dear Reader. If these words remind you of something, follow up on a line of inquiry into your own consciousness. That would be the ideal, in my estimation.

And remember, these collaborations take place during sleep, primarily, and of course within the Uncommon Trance, the Guided Visualizations, and other Intentional states of consciousness. As you practice consciously communicating with your other lives, it becomes easier to remember this information.

Mark: Seth, what occurs for you when you reminisce about your lives for this project? Are you reliving your lives, or simply remembering the general conditions?

Seth: I am energy at this time, Mark. I am currently composed of light: a Light Body. As such I am quite capable of briefly entering into the mental environment of any one of my many existences. I do not interfere with the consciousnesses of the lives, however, when I do this. It is more of a subtle emphasis. Let me digress for just a moment...

Creative Work

All of you in your system create your individual identities within each moment of Reality Creation. You do this by bringing forward from limitless probabilities the material you require to create your Essential Identity and thus your Personal Reality Field. I have referred to you as artists in this way in my material. You creatively select the essences of personality from all of your Simultaneous Lives. Your system of assessment and decision on what to include in this creative work is determined by your beliefs. Now this is old material here and I will leave it at that. But to answer your question more basically...

I am also a reality creator even though I have achieved Light Body status and am no longer on the reincarnational trajectory on which you and your colleagues find yourselves. I too select from my Simultaneous Lives, Mark, the material required to create MY Essential Identity in the moment. This is how I glean my data for this project. I am etheric matter and I may bring my consciousness within the minds of these other subjects in an unobtrusive way.

You are capable of these types of investigations also. Those of you who explore your Past Lives are doing precisely what I do when I gather material for this autobiography. In the etheric world, the Telepathic Network, it is possible for any one of my gifted students to gather material and write YOUR OWN multidimensional autobiography. I expect that some of you will do just that in the very near future. Does this answer your question, Mark?

Mark: Yes, and thanks for elaborating.

Seth: You are welcome. Now let us complete this book and send the reader on their way.

Epilogue

I sincerely hope that you have found something of value in our brief little survey. Now, the object here seems to be, in my view, to read and to simply let the information settle within your consciousness. Associations are then made naturally, you see. Some of this activity is conscious, in that you notice it in your waking reality. But for the most part the associations are made in the so-called "unconsciousness" of the dreamstate, or during meditations, prayer, and so on.

As you move forward in your studies, a resonance is created within your mental environment. By this I mean that, if you allow these ideas to simply BE with you, to find their place within your psyche, the important work is already done. Then, what needs to be revealed to you to help you on your journey, will be revealed. The information comes in the form of inspirations, impulses, and Holographic Inserts. Ideas such as I offer you here in these pages have the power and the potential to help you to transform your life. It is as though one idea stimulates your mental conversation, that then leads to other ideas, other memories, other emotions. In time you may discover that you are, in truth, recovering memories that ARE from other lives. When this occurs you may be stunned and happily surprised by your accomplishment. Let that enlargement of belief serve to motivate you to continue your studies. We call these brief glimpses into the other lives "momentary awakenings." I have shown you how I explore my lives, now you may do the same. Good luck.

Ritual of Sanctuary

The Ritual of Sanctuary was presented to readers in our book on *Soul Evolution* when we first began to emphasize direct exploration of the Unknown Reality. We felt that the reader would require some personalized protection in their experimentation.

The most simple form of the Ritual is to imagine, prior to psychic pursuits, a golden Light surrounding you. Nothing harmful can penetrate this field of Light. It has a healing protective influence. You may certainly use this simplified form while you go about creating your own Ritual.

The object here is to generate positive energies with your creative consciousness. Try listing on a piece of paper your positive beliefs and ideas that denote security, peace, and protection. The next step would be to, perhaps artistically, distill these potent concepts down into an image, statement, or physical object that resonates with the protective energies. Naturally you may include gestures, visualizations, or any other evocative materials. Practice your Ritual until you can create at-will the state of Sanctuary within your own consciousness. Only you will know when you are successful.

Glossary
Definitions for the concepts Seth discusses
in this book.

All That Is - The energy source from which all
life came throughout the multitude of Universes,
transcending all dimensions of consciousness and
being part of all. Also referred to as the Logos and
Evolutionary Consciousness.

Ancient Wisdom - The knowledge of the
magicians, shamans, witches and healers of the
past.

Awakening - As the Ancient Wisdom is
remembered by humanity, an awareness of the
greater reality is experienced by individuals.

Beliefs - Ideas, images, and emotions within your
mental environment that act as filters and norms in
the creation of Personal Realities.

Bleedthroughs - Momentary experiencing of lives
being lived in other timeframes and other systems
of reality.

Co-creation - You co-create your reality with the
limitless creative energies of All That Is.

Consciousness Unit (CU) - The theorized
building blocks of realities. Elements of awarized
energy that are telepathic and holographic.

Courage - Courage and Loving Understanding
replace fear and anger in the creation of Positive
Realities.

Denial - The ego/intellect prevents the learning of
Lessons by denying the truth of the matter.

Dimensions - Points of reference from one reality
to the other with different vibrational wavelengths
of consciousness.

Divine Day - The student attempts to live a complete waking day while maintaining contact with the Energy Personality.

Divine Will - The will is potentiated through ongoing contact and communication with Beings of Light. Also called Intent.

Ego/Intellect - The aspect of the personality that attempts to maintain the status quo reality.

Ecstasy - The positive emotion experienced in contact with the Divine.

Embodiment - Precepts are lived in the creation of improved realities.

Energy Personality - A being capable of transferring their thought energy inter-dimensionally to physical beings and sometimes using the physical abilities of those beings for communication. For example, Seth.

Entity - Being not presently manifested on the physical plane. Also known as a Spirit.

Fourth-Dimensional Shift - Consciousness expands as the individual experiences an awareness of all Simultaneous Existences. Also called Unity of Consciousness Awareness.

Gestalts of Consciousness (GOCs) - Assemblages of Consciousness Units into Reality Constructs of all types.

gods - Consciousness personalized and projected outward into reality. A self-created projection of the developing ego.

Holographic Insert - Teaching aid of the non-physical beings. Multisensory construct experienced with the Inner Senses.

GLOSSARY

Incarnation - To move oneself into another life experience on the physical plane.

Inner Sense - The Soul's perspective. Both the creator and the perceiver of Personal Realities.

Intellectualization - The aspect of the psyche that attempts to figure things out so that the status quo is maintained.

Intention - See Divine Will.

Lessons - Chosen life experiences of the Soul for further spiritual evolution.

Light Body - The etheric body of refined light.

Love - Love with a capital L is the force behind manifestation in the Third Dimension.

Moment Point - The current empowered moment of awakening. Exists as a portal to all points past, present, and future and all Simultaneous Lives.

Mystery Civilizations - Foundational civilizations largely unknown to modern science. Some examples are Atlantis, Lemuria, and GA.

Negative Emotion - Habitual creation of negative emotions creates enduring negative realities.

Negative Entities - Negative energies that roam the Universes in pursuit of their own power to dominate.

Percept - Perception creates reality in the Third Dimension. See *Thought Reality*.

Personal Reality Field - The radius within your self-created world within which you have the most control in the creation of Reality Constructs.

Precept - Empowered concepts of manifestation. Example: you create your own reality.

Reality - That which one assumes to be true based on one's thoughts and experiences. Also called Perceived Reality.

Reality Creation - Consciousness creates reality.

Reincarnational Drama - Soul Family drama enacted to teach the participants a Lesson in Value Fulfillment.

Scientist of Consciousness - The researcher studies the phenomena within the Personal Reality Field by testing hypotheses in experimentation. See Precept.

Observer Perspective - Self-created aspect of consciousness that sees beyond the limitations of the ego/intellect. An intermediary position between the ego and the Soul Self.

Seth - An energy personality essence that has appeared within the mental environments of humans throughout the millennia to educate and inspire.

Simultaneous Lives - The multidimensional simultaneous experiences of Souls in incarnation.

Soul - The non-physical counterpart to the physical human body, personality, and mentality. The spiritual aspect of the human.

Soul Evolution - The conscious learning of Lessons without denial or intellectualization.

Soul Family - The group of humans you incarnate with lifetime after lifetime to learn your Lessons together.

Spiritual Hierarchy - Beings of Light who have mastered multidimensional levels of experience throughout the Universes and have moved on to higher service in the evolution of all Souls.

GLOSSARY

The Christ - The embodiment of The Christ
in your World. Also called World Teacher. First
described in *Seth Speaks*.

The Council - Members of the Spiritual Hierarchy.
Highly evolved beings that advise Souls on
incarnations for their spiritual evolution.

The New World - The Positive Manifestation.

The Vanguard - Advocates for humanity and
Mother Earth who incarnate together to lead
progressive movements of various kinds.

Third Dimension - The physical plane of Earthly
existence.

Trance State - The relaxed, focused state of
awareness that allows the Scientist of Consciousness to conduct experiments and collect data.

Value Fulfillment - Consciousness seeks
manifestation of itself into all realities via the
fulfillment of all values.

Visionary - Reincarnated magicians, shamans,
witches and healers in this current timeframe.

I think we're going to have to do a book or two or three or four or many more to get the masses to see the problem ... Seth

More Books?

Seth has promised to continue to communicate with us to further the awakening of humanity. This means that there will be an ongoing source of current, inspirational messages available from: **Seth Returns Publishing**

Communications from Seth on the Awakening of Humanity

9/11: The Unknown Reality of the World
The first original Seth book in two decades.

The Next Chapter in the Evolution of the Soul
The Scientist of Consciousness Workbook.

Thought Reality - Healing Regimen/Spiritual Prosperity

The Trilogy - Three New Seth Books to Inspire You

All That Is - Seth Comments on the Creative Source
Mystery Civilizations - Seth Answers Reader's Questions on Legendary Civilizations
Soul Mate/Soul Family - Contains Soul Mate Project

Seth - A Multidimensional Autobiography
Resonance - Manifesting Your Heart's Desire in 2011
Seth on Death and the Afterlife in 2012

To order, visit **sethreturns.com** or **amazon.com** or ask your local bookstore to carry the new Seth books.